Along The Coast
Pennan to St Fergus

By
Stanley Bruce

Published by
BARD BOOKS
On behalf of the
Banffshire Maritime & Heritage Association

Photography by
Stanley Bruce
(Unless otherwise stated)

© Copyright Stanley Bruce 2009.

First Edition.

ISBN 978-0-9547960-9-9

This edition published in 2009 by Bard Books on behalf of the Banffshire Maritime & Heritage Association.
All proceeds from the sale of this book will go to the Banffshire Maritime & Heritage Association.

www.banffshiremaritime.org.uk

Printed by Cooper Printers, Fraserburgh.

Contents

Fraserburgh - The Broch,
Rosehearty - Rossachdair,
Pennan - Auchmedden,
Breathe, the salt air.

Introduction - The wonderful coastline between Pennan and St Fergus has been called many names, including 'The land at the bend in the ocean', and 'The land of the cow', both which are still very appropriate today. Our journeys start Pennan which sits nestled below the rugged cliffs on the Moray Firth shore is a complete contrast to our final destination St Fergus, which stands aside one of the longest beaches in Europe, stretching seventeen kilometres from St Combs to Peterhead; backed in places with sand dunes up to seventy-five feet high. Amazingly I've spent an afternoon on this beach at Rattray Head and not seen a soul. The only reason I can give for this, is that the access road is poor, and it's not easy to find without a map.

There are many place names in Buchan particularly along the coast which reflect Pictish times, and on this stretch within a few miles of each other are Pitsligo, Pitullie, and Pittendrum. Pit is likely to mean good arable or pastoral land - a farm. Of course the Pict's worked the land, but they also fished the sea, and used many of the Buchan beaches as natural harbours. The leader of the Pict's was the Mormaer, and what better place for the Mormaer leader of Buchan to live than on Mormond Hill (Mormaer's Hill?). From the summit of the hill the whole of Buchan can be seen. Which raises the question did the Romans defeat the Pict's here in 84AD? We may never know, but we do know that Buchan has been inhabited as far back as 3000BC by the Beaker Folk, evidence of their existence has been found at many places including Rathen, Memsie, and at Upper Boyndlie Farm.

Buchan is rich in heraldry, and the Buchan lairds kept the stone masons busy carving armorial panels for their castles, big houses, and gravestones, of which, several examples can be seen in this book.

The largest town on this stretch of the coast is Fraserburgh which expanded greatly during the herring boom years of the 19th century, and today is still one of the biggest fishing ports in Scotland. The town's Heritage Centre and the Lighthouse Museum are both well worth a visit.

While walking along the coast not so long ago a man asked me "Is there anything on today?" He was looking for a planned event, unfortunately there was nothing planned for that particular day, however the coast is open everyday, and to my mind there's always something to see if you know where to look. In this book you won't find any great exaggerations about the places mentioned as commonly used in the media today, I tell it exactly as it is, and I believe that is very important, as long as the weather is good you will see the Buchan coast as you see it in this book.

Stanley Bruce, BSc, I.Eng, MIMarEST.
Chairman, Banffshire Maritime & Heritage Association.

Pennan – We start our journey at the beautifully secluded hamlet of Pennan in the parish of Aberdour. The hamlet was established on land that was considered not much good for anything else. Many of the houses are painted and built gable end to the sea to protect them from the elements.

Pennan is the most westerly village in the pre 1975 county of Buchan (Not Banffshire as claimed by some). Pennan once famous for its mill stones, which were once quarried here and precariously rolled down the hill to the harbour for transportation is nowadays more famous for its association with the 1983 film 'Local Hero'.

Pennan Harbour (Category 'B' listed).

The red phone box featured in the film is reputed to be the most dialled-into phone box in the whole of Scotland. Fishermen used to land their catch in the small harbour but like the other small fishing villages in the North East when the larger steam drifter fishing boat was introduced in the early 1900's the fishermen of Pennan re-located to the larger harbours such as Fraserburgh and Macduff. Pennan is now very popular with tourists who come here to relax in a stress-free environment. Many in the past have enjoyed refreshments, and hospitality in the Pennan Inn, but it is currently closed, so bring a packed lunch with you because the nearest shop is 4 mile away in Gardenstown.

The hamlet of Pennan, looking eastwards from Fort Fiddes.

*We shall now travel back-up the steep road to the crossroads at the top of the hill. To the left we can see **Auchmedden Church**.*

Auchmedden Church – Auchmedden is the old name for Pennan and is derived from St Medden (St Medan) who first built a church here. Auchmedden Church built in 1884 stands on the B9031 at the top of the village. I read an interesting piece of information regarding this church in the December 1987 edition of 'The Scots Magazine' it showed a photograph of a book-case in the church with about one hundred books in it. This book-case complete with approximately three hundred books was donated by

Auchmedden Church.

James Coats junior (1841 to 1912) of J. & P. Coats Ltd. of Paisley the famous thread makers. Coats donated book-cases complete with books to all of the Scottish lighthouses, and to many of the small villages all around Scotland.

*Follow the B9031 east, which is twisty and often steep and you come to the village of **New Aberdour**.*

New Aberdour - The planned village of New Aberdour was founded in 1798. In the grounds of the parish church built in 1818 stands the parish war memorial, and there is also an interesting old but badly weathered sundial on the south facing wall of the church.

Sundial at New Aberdour Church.

*Back-track westward and take the first unclassified road on the right heading down to the coast, turn left at the T junction and **St Drostan's Church** is located behind a large house which used to be the church manse.*

South of St Drostan's church is a footpath which leads along the cliffs west to Pennan. Along this stretch of the coast there is a cave in the bay of 'Nethermill of Auchmedden'. According to legend the cave was entered by a piper, who was heard playing 'Lochaber no more', as he entered the cave the music faded, and he was never seen again.

St Drostan's Church – The ruined church we see today is a 16th century church re-built in 1760; however an earlier 6th century church possibly one of the earliest in the north east of Scotland is said to have existed around here. It may have been sited here or perhaps on the promontory a little further east where the remains of **'Dundarg Castle'** can be seen. The church is dedicated to St Drostan who landed here with his uncle St Columba in 580A.D. St Drostan went on to become the 'Abbot of Deer Abbey', which is approximately ten miles south east. St Drostan is mentioned in 'The Book of Deer' a tenth century manuscript which was written by the monks of Deer

Doo-cot at St Drostan's Church, Aberdour.

Abbey. This book is thought to be the earliest Gaelic manuscript in existence, and is currently held in Cambridge University, perhaps one day it will be returned to the north east. You can see the book and find out more about it at www.bookofdeer.co.uk. Also in the church you can see an ancient stone baptismal font thought to date back to the 6th century. Adjacent to the church is a very unusual and small doo-cot (dove-cot) which may have been built using masonry from the church. Buried in the church-yard are the 'Baird's of Auchmedden' the local lairds, they retained the lands of Auchmedden for upwards of three centuries from approximately 1430 to 1750. Grid Ref NJ884644.

'Thomas the Rhymer' wrote the following verse:

"As long as eagles nested on the cliffs of Pennan, there would be Baird's in Auchmedden."

St Drostan's Ancient Baptismal Font.

St Drostan's Church, Aberdour.

*Carry on down the road towards the coast to **Aberdour Beach**.*

Aberdour Beach – This wonderful beach is very popular with locals and visitors alike. The pebble beach with nearby caves cut in the red sandstone cliffs are well worth a visit. Whether you want to explore the caves or paddle in the beach; on a beautiful summer's day you could quite easily imagine yourself somewhere on the Mediterranean.

Cave at Aberdour Beach.

Aberdour Beach looking west to Strahangles Point.

Jane Whyte Memorial – Situated to the west of the beach car park, across the stream is a memorial plaque sited in the remains of a gable end of a cottage known as 'Waulkmill'. The sea has always played at major part in the lives of the Buchan folk, and many a heroic deed has been recorded along this coast over the years. Here at Aberdour Beach the ship 'William Hope' ran aground 28th October 1884 and Jane Whyte who lived in this cottage entered the sea and

Jane Whyte Memorial, Aberdour Beach.

she managed to get a line to the stricken ship, and saved the lives of fifteen men. The RNLI awarded her their silver medal and £10. The plaque was erected in 1986 to commemorate the event. Grid Ref NJ884647.

8

A little to the east of the car park is a well dedicated to St Drostan:

St Drostan's Well – This holy well dedicated to St Drostan is said to have once given 'Wondrous cures', however today it is considered 'Unfit for human consumption' so don't try it! The upper part of the well features a Victorian pink granite basin and cover carved with a scallop shell motif, which bears the inscription "St Drostan's Well 1884', this was erected by J. Findlater LLD, a native of Aberdour. Grid Ref NJ887647.

St Drostan's Well.   *Upper part of St Drostan's Well.*

Head back up the road and follow the unclassified road eastwards, and about ½ a mile to the east you will see a fine looking castellated house, and adjacent to this you will see a promontory which has the remains of a stone built gateway which was once the gateway to Dundarg Castle:

Dundarg Castle – Perhaps once a Pict settlement or even the site of St Drostan's 6th century chapel, Dundarg today remains mysterious. The castle of Dundarg (The red fort) once stood on this red sandstone promontory but all that remains today is part of the gateway. The Comyn castle was destroyed in 1308 during Bruce's 'Harrying of Buchan', however in 1333 Henry de Beaumont (<1285 to 1340) 4th Earl of Buchan who fought at Bannockburn for the English, an ally of King Edward II of England and heir of John Comyn (<1260 to 1308) 3rd Earl of Buchan through marriage, rebuilt it for his own use anticipating a new invasion of Scotland by the English. Regent Sir Andrew Murray (1297 to 1338) the Guardian of Scotland captured the castle in 1334, and it is said that he was the first person to use cannons to attack a Scottish castle; he must have been impressed with the cannons because it appears that he almost completely destroyed it. William Douglas Simpson (1896 to 1968), historian and archaeologist headed an archaeological excavation at Dundarg 1950 – 1951. There was also an excavation in 1981. Grid Ref: NJ895648.

Access to the castle is through private land so please ask at the house if you intend to visit it.

The promontory of Dundarg Castle looking from the south.

In the Marischal Museum, Aberdeen there is a point from a prehistoric 'Ard-share' (A primitive plough), found at 'Dundarg Castle' by William Simpson during his 1951 dig. The 'Ard-share' made of oak is likely to have been used by very early farmers and it was used to cut a narrow channel in the ground rather than turning it over. The seeds would then have been planted in the channel and covered with earth.

Dundarg Castle Gate Tower.

*We now head further eastwards passing **Cowshaven**, **Egypt**, and the **Witching Steen**.*

<u>**RAF Bombing Range**</u> - An RAF bombing range was established between Aberdour and Rosehearty in the early 1950's. It was closed in 2000, and the control tower in **Rosehearty** built in 1994 complete with bombproof glass was sold, and converted to a house. (See page 16).

<u>**Lord Pitsligo's Cave**</u> – There is a cave (Now blocked) on the coast at Cowshaven with this name, and it was just one of the many hiding places used by the illusive **Alexander Forbes 4th Lord Pitsligo** (1678 to 1762) after the 'Battle of Culloden', see page 14 for more information. Grid Ref NJ913663.

10

Egypt – You may find 'Egypt' a strange name to be associated with Buchan but a farm exists not far from the coast between New Aberdour and Rosehearty with this very name. The farm owners must find it amusing because they have a camel on their sign. On the coast, north of the farm are the remains of some old Ice House's.

Follow the road east and you come to a 'T' junction if you look inland and westward you will see a large stone (Steen in Doric) standing prominently on the top of the hill known locally as the 'Witching Steen'.

Egypt Farm sign.

The Witching Steen - The 'Witching Steen' sits in a drystane dyke high on a hill about two miles south west of **Rosehearty**, this is where the gallows once stood and where witches and criminals were once hanged. A local man said he remembers the gallows still visible in the 1960's. Interestingly the last person to be sentenced to death in Scotland was Patrick McCarron in 1964 for fatally shooting his wife, he didn't actually make it to the gallows he hanged himself in prison in 1970. Grid Ref NJ919655.

*Looking eastward you will see the **Mounthooly Doo-cot**, the finest one in all of Buchan.*

The Witching Steen.

Mounthooly Doo-cot – The doo-cot (dove-cot) was built by Lord Garden of Gardenstown (Or Troup) in 1800 when he purchased the Pitsligo Estate. The name means 'Holy Mount' implying earlier Christian associations. Inside it has nesting boxes for three hundred pigeons. The castellated top of the doo-cot is beautifully finished off with twelve ball finials. About halfway up the outside of the walls is the usual rat ledge purposely kept below the entrance for the birds to keep vermin out. In the 18th and 19th centuries pigeons were kept for their meat which was eaten during the winter months; they were easy to keep because they foraged around to the despair of many farmers for

Mounthooly Doo-cot.

11

their own food. It wasn't until Vice-Admiral John Hamilton-Leslie (1679 to 1722) 9th Earl Rothes introduced the 'neep' (turnip) from Europe that cattle and sheep could be wintered in Buchan, prior to this they were taken south for the winter. There is a picnic area with parking adjacent to the doo-cot. The doo-cot is category 'A' listed by Historic Scotland. Grid Ref NJ924659.

*Follow the road east and take the next turning on the left to **Peathill Old Kirk**.*

Peathill Old Kirk – Legend tells us that Alexander Forbes (1st Lord Forbes of Pitsligo) was so annoyed with the minister of **Aberdour** who when delivering his sermon ranted on against Pitullie, Pittendrum and Pitsligo calling them the 'Three Pits of Hell' that he stormed out of the church vowing to build his own church. This he duly did at his own expense in 1632, and on 28th June 1633 an act of parliament separated the parish of Pitsligo from that of Aberdour. The stones for the bell-cote are believed to have been imported from the Netherlands in 1635, and legend also tells us that when the stones arrived Lord Pitsligo was seriously ill and bedridden, however he had

Peathill Old Kirk Bell-cote of 1635.

instructed his servants and local mason to build-up the bell-cote in the courtyard of **Pitsligo Castle** where he could see them for himself before they were erected on his fine new kirk. They must have been to his satisfaction otherwise he would have not ordered its erection. The church was a prominent landmark from the sea and was known locally as the 'Visible Kirk'. On the wall below the bell-cote is a heraldic panel with a quartered shield containing the three boar's heads from the family crest of the Forbes' of Pitsligo, and three rosettes of the Fraser's of Philorth. On the outside of the kirk on the south wall is a remarkably well preserved heraldic panel of Alexander Forbes 1st Lord Forbes of

Heraldic Panel of Alexander 1st Lord Forbes of Pitsligo. Peathill Old Kirk.

Pitsligo dated 1634 with symbols of mortality. Inside the kirk is the Forbes family vault. Like many of the old kirks this kirk had been altered several times before being replaced by the adjacent much larger church in 1890. The new church also uses the bell from the original kirk and the wonderful wood Jacobean carved aisle known as the 'Forbes Loft'. Sadly the roof of the old kirk was removed by the local council in the 1960's. The bell-cote of the old kirk was restored by Aberdeenshire Council in 2003 as part of their 'Historic Kirkyards Project' and further work is pending. The kirk is category 'A' listed by Historic Scotland. Grid Ref NJ934663.

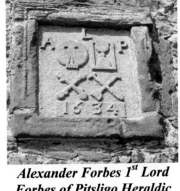

Alexander Forbes 1st Lord Forbes of Pitsligo Heraldic Panel, Peathill Old Kirk.

Grave slab - kilted angels resurrection scene.

Peathill Old Kirk (Later church in the background).

In the kirkyard there is a very unusual grave slab which shows a resurrection scene of Jesus with a crown, standing above a skull and bones, flanked with two kilted angels; this slab is to the memory of Anna Sim (AS) spouse of William Ranney (WR), she died in 1724. A stone effigy and the initials C.A. were once visible on the east gable of the church. These may have been the initials of the builder of the church Charles Allan, or these could be the initials of Andrew Cant (1590 to 1663), he was the first ever minister of Pitsligo Parish from 1633 to 1638, and was known as 'Canting Andrew'. Cant was a Presbyterian minister, and leader of the Scottish Covenanters. In 1639 he sat in the General Assembly at Glasgow which abolished episcopacy in Scotland. His son Andrew Cant became the principal of Edinburgh University.

Pitsligo Parish Church - Built in 1890 to the design of Alexander Marshall McKenzie (1848 to 1933) of Elgin. Incorporates the Jacobean Aisle of 1634 from the old kirk, and the bell dated 1798. Category 'A' listed by Historic Scotland mainly due to the Jacobean Aisle.

We will now follow the road heading north a short distance to **Pitsligo Castle.**

Pitsligo Castle – Pitsligo Castle was built in 1424 by Sir William Forbes (1385 to 1446) of Kinaldy, when he acquired the estate through marriage to Agnes Fraser (c1400 to c1460) the daughter of Sir William Fraser (1377 to 1441) of Philorth in 1423. The Forbes family extended it in the 1550's to 1570's. The last occupier of Pitsligo Castle was **Alexander Forbes, 4th Lord Forbes of Pitsligo**; he was a fervent Jacobite supporter who fought at Culloden in 1746, and for this he spent the rest of his life on the run from the English. He had many hiding places in Buchan including the cave at **Cowshaven.** He was known by the locals as 'Sanny Brown' a tramp, and this disguise served him well often evading capture by the skin of his teeth. He died 21st December

Alexander Forbes, 2nd Lord Forbes of Pitsligo, and Lady Mary Erskine - Armorial Panel 1663.

1762, and it is said that he was liked so much that thousands attended his funeral. In 1989 the castle was bought by Alexander Forbes a descendant of Malcolm Forbes the American multi-millionaire publisher of Forbes Magazine. Alexander Forbes had renovations executed to secure the structure of the building prior to his death in February 1990. Pitsligo Castle is currently owned by the Pitsligo Castle Trust who are working with Historic Scotland to find £600,000 to commence restoration work. The NE corner of Scotland is rich in heraldry and three fine examples can be seen here at Pitsligo Castle. The 'Friends of Pitsligo Castle' have talked about Pitsligo Castle

King James VI, pre-Union of the Crowns - Armorial Panel 1577.

being restored and a Jacobite and Heraldry Centre being sited here. To my mind the Pict's of the north east would also be another appropriate theme for any display at the castle. The castle is category 'A' listed by Historic Scotland. Please note the grounds of the castle are private, and the castle itself dangerous; so please observe from a safe distance. Grid Ref NJ937669.

James VI of Scotland and England - Armorial Panel. 1603 Union of the Crowns.

Pitsligo Castle.

*We will now drive the short distance northwards, down the hill to **Rosehearty**.*

<u>Rosehearty</u> – The name has two possible Gaelic derivatives 'Rossachdair' the anchorage ground near the promontory or 'Ross' meaning promontory, and 'Ard' meaning a height. The settlement is said to have been established by shipwrecked Danes in the 14th century, however an earlier Pict settlement is thought to have existed here. Although not recorded it is easy to imagine that the Vikings visited Rosehearty long before the 14th century, battles have been recorded at Gardenstown to the west 1004 A.D., and at Cruden Bay to the east 1012 A.D. It was Alexander Forbes (d.1690) 2nd Lord Forbes of Pitsligo who did the needful to make Rosehearty a burgh of barony 13th July 1681.

Cairn / War Memorial Rosehearty.

Forbes then built a new seatown for the fisher folk. In the mid 19th century the harbour prospered due to the boom times of the herring fishing, and had up to eighty-eight boats. In 1865 the railway came to Fraserburgh and Rosehearty Harbour suffered without a rail link, and by the 1880's the fishermen were landing their catch in Fraserburgh. Plans were made to run a line to Rosehearty, but they came to nothing. Today the harbour holds around a dozen small boats, fishing mainly with lobster creels.

Rosehearty has its own golf course on the eastern edge of the village, which has reasonable green fees. The coast here is very popular with divers, reason being there are several shipwrecks lying near the coast and the water is very clear. The most noted wrecks are the 'SS Fram' which was sunk by a German U-Boat 1st February 1940, the 'Prestonian' and the 'Noordpool'.

However the most famous wreck is the 'Edward Bonaventure' which was wrecked here in 1556, she was carrying Ossip Gregorevitch Nepeja the 1st Russian Ambassador to England of the Tsar Ivan IV (Ivan the Terrible), and precious items such as gold, silver, furs, and jewels. The locals are said to have looted the wrecked ship, and Queen Mary I (1516 to 1558) instructed that all looted items were to be returned, but only items of low value and wax were returned.

Ex RAF observation Tower now converted to a house.

Another tale of rescue occurred here when a German boat called the 'Maria' ran aground here in 1904, it's said that Mr Shirran the banker's dog Don took a line out to the ship in his mouth and all onboard were saved. For this daring deed the dog was awarded a silver collar. Rosehearty once had its own outdoor swimming pool, but this has long since been filled-in.

Rosehearty Harbour. (Category 'B' listed by Historic Scotland).

We shall now head east along the B9031 and take the first single track road on the right after the golf course to Pitullie Castle.

Pitullie Castle – The castle is situated one mile east of Rosehearty, and was built by Alexander Fraser (c1570 to 1636) 9th laird of Philorth in 1596, and it was last occupied around 1850. Alexander Fraser married Margaret Abernethy (1609 to 1669) of Saltoun in 1595, and it is likely that the castle was built for the couple; as a result of this marriage the Fraser's inherited the Saltoun peerage. The Fraser's gave up Pitullie in the 1690's. Above the doorway there was once heraldic panels but these are now gone. Currently there doesn't seem to be any restoration or even consolidation planned for the castle, where is Historic Scotland? Category 'A' listed. Grid Ref NJ945670.

Pitullie Castle. (As viewed from the north east).

Pitullie / Sandhaven – Pitullie is one example of a 19th century Scottish fishing village with many of the houses standing gable end to the sea, however it is thought that fishermen lived here as far back as the 16th century and perhaps even earlier as a Pict settlement. Pitullie has a small natural harbour suitable for small boats. Connected to the east of Pitullie is the village of Sandhaven. Sandhaven Harbour was established in 1840 with the erection of the west pier. In the 1870's further piers were added, and it was around this time that the building of houses in the village took off. The once thriving harbour with up to one hundred fishing boats and several herring curing yards now has crumbling walls, and the once flourishing boatyard of J. & G. Forbes & Co. is closed although the yard buildings still stand today. The launchways in the picture below have now been recently taken away. The most famous boat to be built here is the Fraserburgh registered 'Fifie' FR958 'Reaper'. She was built in 1901 and has been beautifully restored by the Scottish Fisheries Museum, in Anstruther, and is often seen at the 'Scottish Traditional Boat Festival' held annually at Portsoy thirty-five mile westward. J. & G. Forbes were in business from around 1900 to 1992, with their last boat the 'Fruitful Vine' being built in 1989; the company had boatyards in both Sandhaven and Fraserburgh.

A Roman coin was found on the beach at Muckhills between Sandhaven and Fraserburgh. Coventry Museum identified it as a151 AD to 154 AD Sestertius of Antoninus Pius (86 to 161 AD).

BF240 Fruitful Vine.

The closed yard of J. & G. Forbes & Co. (Boat-builders) Ltd, Sandhaven.

FR958 Fifie 'Reaper' & sign at Fraserburgh Harbour in 2005.
(The sign has since been taken down).

*On the south eastern outskirts of the village is the **Mains of Pittendrum**:*

Mains of Pittendrum – This is a three storey Laird's House built in 1734 by George Cumine, and the Cumine coat-of-arms is proudly displayed above the door. Currently privately owned, and category 'A' listed by Historic Scotland. Grid Ref NJ964671.

Mains of Pittendrum, Sandhaven.

Sandhaven Meal Mill – The mill was built in the 19th century and was driven by a large water wheel on the east gable of the building. Inside you can see how oatmeal used to be ground. The weather vane has a pig on it, and the reason for this is that the owner of the mill kept pigs which were fed on the residue from the oats. The mill is owned by the Aberdeenshire Council but at the time of publication of this book it was sadly closed until further notice. Category 'B' listed by Historic Scotland.

Weather Vane.

Waterwheel at the Sandhaven Meal Mill.

*We now head further eastward to **Fraserburgh**:*

Mill Sign.

On the outskirts of the town are unmarked graves where the dead from the shipwrecked **'Edward Bonaventure'** were buried. Due to their dark skin colour the Fraserburgh folk of the time didn't want them buried in their cemetery. Unfortunately the graves are not marked so the exact location today is unknown but it is thought to be near where the Gut Factory once stood.

Entering Fraserburgh (Locally known as 'The Broch') we will first stop at the village of Broadsea, which can be found by taking George Street, the first road on the left after the pelican crossing, and then a right at the T junction at the bottom.

Broadsea – Broadsea today is encircled by the town of Fraserburgh, but it wasn't always so, Broadsea used to be a thriving village community in its own right. Referred to as the seatown, it was home to many fishermen and their families. The fishermen of Broadsea used to haul their small un-decked boats onto the beach, and I can remember small boats here in the 1970's. Broadsea at one time had its own school, shop, hall, and its own post office which closed in 2008. Broadsea is now a conservation area. If you're interested in genealogy then search in Yahoo under groups using Fraserburgh, and you'll see the following photograph; the members of this group have a vast amount of information on the families of Broadsea, Fraserburgh and beyond.

Broadsea.

Broadsea was home to Christian Watt (1833 to 1923) her memories of her life in Broadsea are recorded in the 'Christian Watt Papers' published in 1983, ISBN 0862280478. The book gives a fascinating insight into the people of Broadsea and how hard life was during her lifetime.

A typical Broadsea fisher cottage.

20

Also published is a book by Broadsea born Jessie N. Bremner titled Jessie's Vision, which also gives an interesting insight into the area.

We now head further eastward to the town centre of ***Fraserburgh.***

<u>Fraserburgh</u> – The town was originally known as Faithlie, however in 1592 Alexander Fraser (c1536 to 1623) 8th laird of Philorth re-named it Fraser's burgh after his family. Many locals didn't like the name change and referred to the town simply as 'The Broch' which is Scottish for burgh. A basin in the harbour and a street today retains the Faithlie name. At Kinnaird Head the towns most north easterly point stands Kinnaird Castle which was built in 1570 also by Alexander Fraser the 8th laird. It was converted in 1787 into the first lighthouse on the Scottish mainland, and in 1995 to a museum. The Town Hall in Broad Street was built in 1853-5, and on which stands the statue of Alexander George Fraser (1785 to 1853) 17th Lord Saltoun proudly overlooking the Broad Gate. He fought in Waterloo in 1815 and was known by the Duke of Wellington as the 'Waterloo Saltoun'. 'The Broch' as it is known to locals is predominately a fishing port with a daily early morning fish market.

The Net, Broad Street, Fraserburgh.

Fraser Mausoleum and the Temperance Fountain, Broad Gate, Fraserburgh.

The Net sculpture in Broad Street, Fraserburgh was created by Scottish artist David Annand, and was erected in 1998 at a cost of £45,000. The sculpture depicts the fish most commonly caught by local fishermen.

In the Broad Gate adjacent to the Old Parish Church is a Mausoleum which was built by the Fraser's Lords Saltoun after the death of Sir Alexander Fraser 8th laird of Philorth (c1536 to 1623). It was until 1944 the burial place of their family.

Alexander Fraser of Abernethy, 14th Lord Saltoun (1710 to 1751).

Alexander Fraser 8th laird of Philorth (c1536 to 1623).

Alexander Fraser 9th laird of Philorth (c1579 to 1636) and his 2nd wife Isabel Gordon.

Coats of arms on the three sides of the Fraser Mausoleum, Broad Gate.

On three sides of the mausoleum are coats of arms (armorial panels) all weathered, but still saveable if action is taken to preserve them soon, and what a feature they could be if restored and painted.

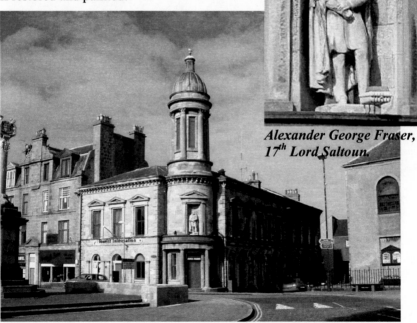

Alexander George Fraser, 17th Lord Saltoun.

Town Hall, Broadgate, Fraserburgh.

22

Fraserburgh Mercat Cross - In the town centre the Mercat Cross stands in a prominent position. This cross dates from 1603, but its appearance today is a shadow of its former self. According to the New Statistical Account of Scotland (1845) the cross stood 23 feet tall on a structure perhaps similar to that of the Mercat Cross in the Castle Gate, Aberdeen. This cross is special because it adorns three coats-of-arms. These are the arms of the Fraser's of Philorth, the Royal Arms of Scotland, and the Scottish version of the early 17th century arms of the United Kingdom (1603 - Union of the Crowns).

Mercat Cross, Fraserburgh.

Fraserburgh has many famous sons, and you can find out about most of them in the Heritage Centre. Fraserburgh born Thomas Blake Glover (1838 to 1911) is probably the most famous. He spent many years in Japan, and is famous for establishing their first shipyard which later became the industrial giant Mitsubishi. He also established a mining company, and a brewery now known as Kirin Beer. He also helped the foundation of the Japanese Navy by importing ships built by Alexander Hall & Co., Aberdeen. He was the first non-Japanese man to be awarded the Order of the Rising Sun. His mansion house still stands in Nagasaki, and is today Japan's greatest tourist attraction, with 1.8 million visitors per annum. The house he bought at 79 Balgownie Road, Bridge of Don, Aberdeen, is now also open as a museum.

Glover with the 'Order of the rising sun'. (Photo courtesy of Adam Leiper Aberdeen).

Another interesting connection is with Newcastle United FC – Fraserburgh in 1910 due to the herring fishing connections received Newcastle's old strip, and have worn black and white ever since.

*We will now head to the north end of the harbour to the wonderful **Museum of Scottish Lighthouses**.*

23

The Museum of Scottish Lighthouses – Kinnaird Head Castle was built in 1570 by Alexander Fraser (c1536 to 1623) 8th laird of Philorth, as a home close to his newly created harbour and town. The Northern Lighthouse Board in 1787 purchased the castle and converted it to the first lighthouse built on the mainland of Scotland. An interesting point to note is that there is no land between here and the Arctic. The lighthouse operated until 1991 when its unmanned replacement was commissioned. Today the castle is part of the museum which also consists of a large building housing many lighthouse artefacts, a shop, and a café. Category 'A' listed.

Kinnaird Head Castle Lighthouse and the Wine Tower.

Fraserburgh Foghorn – As a child I remember the drone of this horn keeping me awake many a night. It was built in 1903 and decommissioned in 1987. It is now also part of the Lighthouse Museum.

Fraserburgh Foghorn.

Wine Tower – The Wine Tower three stories high was also built by Alexander Fraser c1570, it was home to the castle's wine cellar, and the laird is thought to have entertained his guests here. The top floor is thought to have once been used as a chapel by the laird's wife Magdalene Ogilvie (b.c1541) of Dunlugas near Turriff. Category 'A' listed.

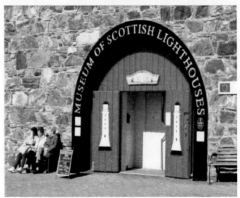

Fraserburgh Lighthouse Museum. (Opened in 1995).

24

Legend of the Wine Tower - Legend tells us that the daughter of the laird had fallen in love with a servant piper, and that the laird was not happy about this. So to separate the two the laird had the piper tied-up in the cave under the tower known as Selches Hole (Seals Hole). The laird then locked-up his daughter in the uppermost floor of the tower (The chapel). Unfortunately for the servant there was an abnormally high tide and the poor man drowned. When the laird's daughter was informed of her lover's fate, she was distraught and committed suicide by jumping from the top of the tower onto the rocks below. The rock that she fell on is still painted red to this day. When the weather is bad it is said that you can hear the skirl of the pipes being played by the ghost of the piper for his lost love.

The Wine Tower is the oldest building in Fraserburgh, and in its upper floor there are seven armorial carved pendants.

In the South Church there is a very old carved stone of 1613 known as the Moses Stone. This stone depicts Moses and the Ten Commandments, and is said to have first been located in the chapel of Fraserburgh University.

The Royal Arms of Scotland, pre 1603, in the upper floor of the Wine Tower.

Moses Stone, South Church.

The other six pendants represent:
Marriage of Alexander Fraser 8th laird to Magdalene Ogilvie in 1570.
Arma Christi. (Heraldic arms of Christ).
3 off representing past Fraser's.
1 off representing the Earl's of Mar, and Huntly. (Calvinist and Catholic).

Fraserburgh Heritage Centre – No visit to Fraserburgh would be complete without a visit to the Fraserburgh Heritage Centre which is sited adjacent to the *Museum of Scottish Lighthouses*. Don't be fooled by the attraction of the lighthouse, the façade of the Heritage Centre may be less impressive but it more than makes up for it inside. The centre is housed in a large building (950m^2) which was once a barrel making factory during the herring boom years, and later a foundry for the Consolidated Pneumatic Toolworks (CPT) locally known as the 'Toolies'. The centre opened 4th July 1998, and has won several awards; with the most recent being four stars from 'Visit Scotland'. The centre contains a wide variety of displays including the following:

Thomas Blake Glover.
Gibb's Transport.
Maconochie Brothers Ltd.
Dr David Murison.
Dr Stewart Slessor OBE.
Bill Gibb fashion designer.
The Broch at War, including an
Anderson Shelter.
RNLI.
Coastguard.
The Fraser's.
John Ross in Africa.

Fraserburgh Heritage Centre.

CPT (Consolidated Pneumatic Toolworks).
The Beach Train – the Kessock Knight.
Guglielmo Marconi.
The Broadsea Project.
Broadsea village model of 1861.
Fishing Heritage.
Scott and Yule Boatbuilding.
Fishing boat models.
Fraserburgh Railway.
Fraserburgh 400.
Granny's Attic.
Fraserburgh Cinema.
Benzie and Miller.
A changing annual display.
A Gift Shop,
and much more!

Broadsea Project - Fraserburgh Heritage Centre.

We will now head southwards to ***Fraserburgh Harbour.***

Fraserburgh Harbour - In 1815 herring fishing was established in Fraserburgh and fourteen curers obtained licences. By 1830 the amount of herring boats increased ten fold, and 200 boats filled the harbour during the herring season.

Fraserburgh Harbour 1920's.

Fishing boats in a very calm Fraserburgh Harbour.

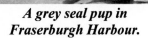

A grey seal pup in Fraserburgh Harbour.

Some build dates
1818 – The South Pier.
1830 – Middle Pier.
1850-56 – Balaclava Pier.
1875-80 – Balaclava Pier extended & the lighthouse erected.
1912-14 – Faithlie Basin.

Fraserburgh Harbour Lighthouse.

*We will now head southwards to the **beach**.*

27

Rescue Services – The first lifeboat in Scotland was established in Fraserburgh in 1806.

Fraserburgh has had many lifeboats through the years, and the heroic deeds of the crews are well recorded. However, the town has also suffered the tragedy of two lifeboat disasters – 'The John and Charles Kennedy' in 1953, with the loss of six lives, and 'The Duchess of Kent' in 1970, with the loss of five lives.

RAF rescue helicopter and the Fraserburgh Lifeboat
'RNLB Willie & May Gall' in Fraserburgh Bay.

Fraserburgh Beach – A little south of the harbour is Fraserburgh Beach, a wonderful three mile stretch backed with fine sand dunes, which is one of the finest beaches in Scotland. At the beach there is a café, and a small Seashore Centre which is open to visitors currently free of charge.

A spectacular December sunrise at Fraserburgh Beach.

Youthful Memories of the Broch Beach
Running down 'Tiger Hill',
Paddling across the 'Kessock Burn',
Standing at the miniature railway,
Patiently waiting for my turn.

Fraserburgh Beach.

At the beach there is also a café and a play-park. There also used to be a small railway but this is now closed, however the restored train the 'Kessock Knight' can be seen in the **Fraserburgh Heritage Centre.**

The restored 'Kessock Knight' train in the Fraserburgh Heritage Centre.

29

We will now leave the beach car-park heading south, then take the first road on the right, then right again at the T junction heading back into town, about 400 yards on the left you will find the Fraserburgh War Memorial.

Fraserburgh War Memorial - Sited at the South Road is the war memorial, which was unveiled 9th Sept 1923. It comprises of a bronze sculpture of a female figure restraining a soldier 'Justice guiding valour' on a large granite base. It commemorates the dead of both WWI (409), and WWII (142). It has a large rectangular granite base with plaques on each face, and built-out small angled corner pieces, the faces of which also bear plaques. The larger figure is a cloaked & seated female (Justice) with a down-turned sword in front of her. To her left side is a smaller figure of a cloaked warrior (Valour) with helmet & shield who is also holding the sword in his left hand. For more information see also www.alexandercarrick.webeden.co.uk.

Fraserburgh War Memorial.

*Drive a little further north and on the right you will see the **Saltoun Water Fountain.***

Saltoun Water Fountain – A wonderful ornate cast iron fountain thought to be the largest and most impressive fountain of this type ever made. Erected in 1904 initially on the site where the war memorial now stands (see the old photo on p31). It was made by the foundry of Walter MacFarlane & Co., Glasgow and has been category 'B' listed since 1993. It was re-sited in its current location when the war memorial was erected in 1923, and painted silver in 1978 to commemorate Queen Elizabeth's Silver Jubilee. Adjacent to the fountain is a play-park known locally as the 'Granddad Swings'.

Fraser coat of arms on the Water Fountain, Saltoun Place, Fraserburgh.

Saltoun Fountain and South Church, Fraserburgh. (Current location).

Saltoun Fountain in its original location, with the Old Parish Church Manse of the time behind. (Postcard one of the 'Adelphi Series' in the 1900's).

*We will now backtrack south and take a left at the roundabout, followed by a right at the next roundabout onto the B9033, immediately on the right you will find the **Kirkton Cemetery**.*

Saltoun Mausoleum, Kirkton - Situated in the cemetery at Kirkton it is a replica of the Fraser Mausoleum in the Broad Gate, Fraserburgh. The Kirkton Mausoleum was erected in 1944. Kirkton is thought to be the site of an ancient settlement much earlier than Faithlie (The original name for Fraserburgh before 1592), St Modan the patron saint of Fraserburgh was the bishop of this settlement, and is known to have had a church here. Early inhabitants are also thought to have been fishermen, and would have pulled their boats up on the nearby beach.

Fraser Mausoleum, Kirkton. (Erected in 1944).

*Follow the B9033 east for ½ mile and you'll find **Fraserburgh Golf Club.***

Fraserburgh Golf Club – Fraserburgh Golf Club was founded in 1777 and is the fifth oldest golf club in Scotland and the seventh oldest golf club in the world; however parish records show golf was being played on Fraserburgh Links as early as 1613. A young lad called John Burnett is recorded as being chastised for playing golf on a Sunday instead of going to church.

Fraserburgh Golf Club. (Tel No 01346 516616)

James Braid professional golfer won the 'British Open Championship' five times and was the runner-up three times between 1901 and 1910, he helped redesign the Fraserburgh course in 1922, and much of it remains the same today. Find out more about the history of golf at Fraserburgh at the **Fraserburgh Heritage Centre**.

*We will now head 1 mile eastwards to the **Waters of Philorth Nature Reserve.***

Waters of Philorth Nature Reserve – Philorth is derived from the Gaelic 'Pool of Orth', 'Orth' meaning stream and the 'Pool' being the area of land north of the castle which was once a pool but its appearance has now changed due to the shifting of the sands and agricultural drainage. It is thought that before these sand dunes formed access was available on the water almost all the way up to a once moated Cairnbulg Castle. Grid Ref NK023647.

Waters of Philorth.

Grey Heron.

*Inland from the reserve is the private residence of **Cairnbulg Castle.***

Cairnbulg Castle – The castle is currently in private hands and is only open to the public by appointment, however you can still see it from a distance. The Comyn Earls of Buchan built the first castle here early in the 14th century (possibly earlier), however it like many other castles in Buchan was destroyed by Robert the Bruce during the 'Harrying of Buchan' in 1308. After the 'Battle of Bannockburn' Bruce gave the lands to William de Ross (d.1372) 3rd Earl of Ross. His daughter Joanna married Alexander Fraser in 1375, thereby becoming the first Fraser's at the 'Manor Place of Philorth' (an early name for the castle). The Fraser's moved to Kinnaird Castle which was built in 1570 - 1571 and sold Cairnbulg Castle in 1611. The next two and a half centuries Cairnbulg changed through many hands and by 1780 it was in ruins. In the late 19th century the Duthie ship-builders and ship-owners from Aberdeen affectionately restored the castle. In 1934 the castle returned to Alexander Arthur Fraser 19th Lord Saltoun (1886 to 1979) head of the Fraser family. The Fraser's have continued the restoration of the castle to this day. Grid Ref NK015639.

Cairnbulg Castle as seen from the north.

Travel eastwards on the B9033 for about ¼ mile and you will see on both sides of the road the remains of RAF Fraserburgh.

<u>RAF Fraserburgh</u> – This airfield opened during WW2 on the 6th December 1941, it was known also known as X6FR. It had three runways, a separate camp called Inverallochy RAF Camp (Known as Tershinty), and a Battle HQ. Today, however all that we see are the scant remains of what was. When it was operational it had 1200 personnel, and was home initially to Spitfire's, and then Warwick's of 279 squadron. During WW2 Fraserburgh was referred to as 'Little London' this was because of the amount of German bombs dropped on the town. The German's flew their bombers out of Trondheim in Norway, which was occupied at the time. From 1903 to 1965 you could have travelled between Fraserburgh and St Combs by rail, it was locally known as the 'Belger Trainnie', Belger being the local name for Cairnbulg.

Inverallochy RAF Camp.

34

*We now travel a little further east and take a left at the crossroads sign-posted to **Cairnbulg** and **Inverallochy,** follow the road north and then westwards and you will come to the two villages.*

Cairnbulg (Belger) and Inverallochy (Wheelick) – These two villages are separated only by a road; together they're locally known as 'Invercairn'.

Cairnbulg Point and Harbour – The east pier of the harbour was built in the 1920's. In the 1980's it was extended and the west pier built using redundant WW2 concrete blocks as foundations for the piers. Plans are afoot to convert the harbour into a twenty berth marina. A beacon stands slightly east of the harbour however this area is notorious for shipwrecks the most recent being the ill-fated Banff registered 'Sovereign' BF380 which ran aground 18th December 2005. Between the harbour and the beacon is a channel cut in the rocks known as the 'Hawse', this channel is used by small boats.

Beacon and a recent shipwreck at Cairnbulg Point (BF380 Sovereign).

Brandesburgh – There used to be a separate village with this name to the east of Cairnbulg, however in 1701 it was incorporated into Cairnbulg village with the name disappearing from use.

Cairnbulg LSA – Shown here is the Cairnbulg LSA (Life Saving Apparatus) housed in the **Fraserburgh Heritage Centre**. This equipment used to be stationed here at Cairnbulg in what is now the white house near the harbour appropriately known as the 'Look Out'. The apparatus was still in use at least until the 1960's.

Cairnbulg LSA.

Maggie's Hoosie, Inverallochy - Maggie's Hoosie, 26 Shore Street, Inverallochy is a typical 'But and Ben' fisher cottage built around 1750. It has been fully restored by the 'Maggie's Hoosie Prevention Trust' and is currently open to the public - June to September, Monday to Thursday 2pm to 4pm or by appointment. When originally built this house would have probably had a turf or thatched roof, not the pan tiled roof we see today. The house is a wonderful example of how the fisher folk lived in the 19th century. Maggie Duthie lived here all her life (1867 to 1950). Maggie died in 1950 and there was no electricity, lighting or heating in the house, she used paraffin lamps, open fires and an antiquated cooking range. The house didn't even have running water Maggie still used the well across the road which had been modernised to include a pump. The cottage was opened to the public 8th June 1966.

Ben – the main living room.   *But – the best or the parlour room.*

Maggie's Hoosie, 26 Shore Street, Inverallochy.

Maggie's Hoosie is open for limited times during May to September; if you plan to visit please phone first - Tel: 01346 514761.

Inverallochy Golf Club – Lying to the east of the village is the eighteen-hole golf course, which was founded in 1888. There is a very nice beach to the north of the course which still has a WW2 pill box. Tel No: 01346 582000.

*We now head back past Inverallochy School and war memorial to the crossroads and turn left onto the B9033, and head towards **Inverallochy Castle** which stands on the right hand side of the road about one mile east.*

36

Inverallochy Castle – Built in 1504, but now stands as a ruin. The castle originally stood adjacent to a loch, and was accessed by a bridge, but the loch has long since been drained, and the land used for agricultural purposes. A stone was once located in a wall of the castle and it read 'I Jurdan Cuming, indwaller here, Gat this hous and lands for biggin the Abbey of Deer'. Translated; 'I Jordan Comyn got this house for building the Abbey of Deer', Jordan was the younger brother of Alexander Comyn (c1217 to c1290) 2nd Earl of Buchan, and is said to have received the lands of Inverallochy for work he carried out on the Abbey. This stone is however thought to have come from an earlier building. The Abbey of Deer was founded 1218 to 1219 under the instruction of William Comyn (1163 to c1233) 1st Earl of Buchan, father of Jordan and Alexander. Grid Ref NK041630.

A spectacular December sunrise at Inverallochy Castle.

Heading a little further east we come to a T junction, turn left into the village of St Combs and Charlestown.

St Combs and Charlestown – The two villages are joined together and are only separated by the Mill Burn. There is no harbour here, and the local fishermen used to pull their small fishing boats onto the beach. The beach stretches southward from St Combs for an amazing seventeen kilometres all the way to Peterhead. At the east end of the village is the old cemetery, and in it stands a small wall – this is all that remains of the church of St Colm built here in 1607. St Combs was established in 1784 to 1785, by Charles Gordon (d.1796) laird of Cairness, and is locally known as the 'New Toon', its residents are known as 'Kwities' or 'New Tooner's'. Charlestown across the 'Mill Water' was established in 1800 to 1801 by a Mrs McKenzie, and was referred to as 'Sodom' by the folk of St Combs.

We will now travel along the B9033 heading south but inland away from the coast. ½ mile south and you will see a sign post to Corsekelly Farm, however we will head further south.

Corsekelly – A Roman head-stud brooch of the period 84 to 90 AD was found here, and inland from here 'Mormond Hill' the only prominent hill in Buchan can clearly be seen. Buchan had many Pictish settlements along the coast, however if I was the Mormaer of Buchan I would have chosen to live on Mormond Hill (Mormaer's Hill?), from here I could oversee all of my lands. To my mind it is possible that the 'Battle of Mons Grapius' occurred here in 84 AD. The Roman army were supported by a fleet of ships and the natural harbour of Rattra (Rattray) 2 mile south would have been an ideal place for the Roman's to land. Rattra is thought to have been visited many times by the Roman's who were in search of its pearls. Tactitus recorded that Calgacus said "Beyond lies no nation, nothing but waves and rocks", true of Mormond Hill but not of other claimed sites of the battle.

Seatown of Corsekelly (Boatlea) – Sited a short distance from the village of St Combs, and oddly half a mile inland from the coast once stood the 'Seatown of Corsekelly' which was locally known as 'Boatlea' or 'Boatley', but nothing exists today. It is thought that the residents were fishermen and farmers.

*2 miles south of St Combs take a right turn at the signpost 'Cairness House' and ¼ mile along this road you will find the gates of **Cairness House.***

Cairness House - Situated four miles south east of **Fraserburgh,** originally on a nine thousand acre estate which included **St Combs** and the **Loch of Strathbeg.** It was built for Charles Gordon (d.1796) between 1791 and 1797 to the design of James Playfair, and is considered one of the finest examples of neoclassical architecture in Britain. Gordon made his fortune in the Jamaican plantations. The house replaced an earlier house of 1781 designed by Robert Burn, which was largely incorporated into the Playfair design. Due to Playfair's death in 1794 Sir John Soane assisted in the final stages of the construction. The house fell into ruin in the 20th century, and in 1991 was recorded as a 'Building at risk' by the Scottish Civic Trust. New owners in 2001 commenced restoration and the house now contains a fine collection of art and furniture, and is open to the public at certain times.' Telephone 01346 582078 if you'd like to visit. See more at: www.cairnesshouse.com. Grid Ref NK038610.

The second laird, Major-General Thomas Gordon (1788 to 1841) was a hero of the Greek Wars of Independence, and wrote a history of the conflict which was published in 1833.

Cairness House.

Sphinx at Cairness House gates.   *Close-up of Sphinx.*

We will now head north along the single track road to the right of the house gates and a short distance on the right is Lonmay Church (1787), and the parish war memorial and a little further Lonmay Old Kirkyard.

Lonmay Old Kirkyard – A pair of weathered heraldic panels on the gate pillars mark the entrance to this ancient kirk-yard. A very interesting fact about this kirk-yard is that the decedents of 'Elvis Pressley' are said to have wed here before immigrating to America. An Andrew Presley married an Elspeth Leg in this kirk-yard in 1713. Researcher Allan Morrison from Greenock said "The first Presley in

Gates to Lonmay Old Kirkyard.

America was a man called Andrew Presley who arrived in North Carolina in 1745" he was the son of Andrew Presley married at Lonmay in 1713. Only a small part of the kirk built in 1607 still stands. This kirk replaced the kirk at St Combs. Lonmay Old kirk was burned to the ground by English soldiers

39

after the battle of Culloden in 1746. The new church was built in 1787. Grid Ref NK039603.

We will now back-track to the B9033, taking a right turn at the T junction. Amongst the trees on the left is Crimonmogate private house and estate, however the house is open for events.

Crimonmogate A mansion house designed by the famous Aberdeen architect Archibald Simpson, and built in 1825 at the expense of the late Patrick Milne who died in 1820. It is generally recognised as Simpson's finest country house. In the grounds is an obelisk erected by Sir Charles Bannerman (1782 to 1851) 8th Baronet of Elsick to the memory of Patrick Milne. Category 'A' listed by Historic Scotland. The house is not open to the public but is available for private functions and corporate days. Grid Ref NK038587. www.cmg-events.co.uk

*We will travel south on the B9033 until we reach the crossroads of the A90, and go straight across for ¾ mile taking the next road on the right. **Berrybrae Stone Circle** stands in the field on the left among a cluster of trees.*

Berrybrae Stone Circle – This stone circle 12.8m x 10.8m diameter dates from 3000BC. However a central ring cairn and three cremation burials have been carbon dated to 1700BC by Aubrey Burl. Currently only the recumbent stone and four uprights are standing out of a total of ten stones. From here the impressive 240ft long Stag of white quartz stone on the south side of 'Mormond Hill' can be seen. Grid Ref NK028572.

Berrybrae Stone Circle.

*We will now back-track to the crossroads of the A90 and turn right. 1 mile on the right is a signpost 'Mintlaw 7', Netherton Farm is the first farm on the right, and behind it is **Netherton Stone Circle.***

Netherton Stone Circle – Sited adjacent to Netherton Farm the circle is a good example of a recumbent stone circle with most of the circle being complete, however it stands amongst a cluster of trees which to my mind spoil the site. I counted sixteen stones. If you intend to visit please ask for permission at Netherton Farm Shop. Grid Ref NK043573.

*We will now head ½ mile east along the A90 to **Crimond**.*

40

Crimond – Village situated on the main road between Fraserburgh and Peterhead (A90). The parish church built in 1812 has a clock with a peculiar mistake on its face where it has sixty-one minutes, six minutes between eleven and twelve, so a day in Crimond lasts twenty-four hours and twenty-four minutes. The clock was donated by the Laing's of Haddo and it is possible that the clock was originally fitted on Haddo House. It was here that Jessie Seymour Irvine composed one of Scotland's best

Crimond Parish Church clock with sixty-one minutes.

hymn's, Psalm 23 'Crimond' (The Lord is my shepherd) she wrote it in 1871. She was the daughter of the Reverend Alexander Irvine of Crimond Parish Church. The parish war memorial stands adjacent to the church.

From the parish church follow the road heading north for ½ mile, and on the right you will come to the Crimond Old Parish Kirkyard.

Crimond Old Parish Kirkyard – Inside the kirkyard are the ruins of the kirk built in 1576, some interesting heraldic panels some weathered others still in good condition, the best preserved being that of William Hay of Wry (Crimogat) dated 1617. There is also a large obelisk in memory of Sir Charles Bannerman (1782 to 1851) 8th Baronet of Elsick and his wife Anne Bannerman (d.1838). Grid Ref NK052576.

W. Hay 1617 Crimond Old Kirkyard.

From the Kirkyard head north, take the 1st road on the right then the 1st road on the left, and follow the road up to the Starnafin Centre, Loch of Strathbeg.

Loch of Strathbeg – Currently a RSPB site and is the largest dune loch in the UK. Strathbeg Bay was once used as a harbour known as 'Starny Keppie' (The port of Buchan) until 1720 when a great storm shifted the sands and it's said a ship was land-locked in the newly formed loch. Such importance was the loch as a trading harbour that two castles guarded it, 'Lonmay Castle'

RSPB Visitor Centre at 'Starnafin' Loch of Strathbeg.

at its northern entrance and 'Rattray Castle' to the south. In 1791 Mr Sellar erected the Savoch wind pump and intended to drain the loch but failed. The nature reserve covers 2300 acres and the loch covers 550 acres and a staggering 252 different species of bird have been recorded here including in the spring pink-footed geese, marsh harriers, and skylarks; in the summer terns, mute swans and great crested glebes; in Autumn pink-footed geese, ruffs and greenshanks, and in the winter the elusive bittern, golden plovers, curlews, lapwings, geese and whooper swans. The reserve has four observation hides where the birds can be seen from, but its worthwhile taking binoculars to get a decent look. www.rspb.org.uk Grid Ref NK057581.

Lonmay Castle – The castle was built by the Comyn Earl's of Buchan and stood at the northern end of Strathbeg, it was destroyed by Robert the Bruce during the 'Harrying of Buchan', today nothing remains.

Back-track to Crimond, and turn left onto the A90 at the Parish Church, follow the A90 east for ½ mile, and take the next road on the left to **Crimond Airfield.**

Crimond Airfield – The aerodrome with its three runways was built during World War II as Royal Navy Air Station, 'RNAS Merganser', and naval air squadron 714 was based here.

Today it remains in the hands of the Ministry of Defence (MoD), and is still in use as a wireless station. The masts which are approximately 900 feet high can be seen from miles around. It was later used during the 'Cold War' (Mid 1940's to early 1990's) to track enemy Soviet submarines. Part of the old airfield is currently used for stock-car

Stock Car Racing Crimond 2007.

racing. Races run bi-weekly during the summer. Grid Ref NK070580.

Back-track to the A90 and turn left, head east and take the next road on the left sign-posted 'Rattray 2', follow this road for 1 mile and take a left at the signpost 'Rattray', about ½ mile on the right you will find **St Mary's Chapel.**

St Mary's Chapel, Rattray – The earliest reference to this chapel is in 1220 when William Comyn (1163 to c1233) 1st Earl of Buchan donated it as alms (A gift to the poor). He is said to have built the chapel in memory of his son who drowned in a well. He later donated money to fund its upkeep, however this site is likely to have been a site of worship dating back as early as the 6th or 7th century. Rattray was created a burgh of Barony in 1564. Grid Ref NK085576.

St Mary's Chapel, Rattray.
(The chapel has since been re-pointed and the Ivy removed).

Castle Hill of Rattray – A Comyn stronghold upgraded in the 13th century probably on the site of an earlier timber fort, it is thought that this site may have been settled as early as 4,500BC. After John Comyn Earl of Buchan was defeated by Robert the Bruce at 'The Battle of Aikey' near Old Deer in 1308 the castle was completely destroyed during the 'Harrying of Buchan'. Grid Ref NK088580. We follow the single track road eastward, this road has deteriorated greatly since the 1970's when the only hazard was drifting sand, and today we are grateful for a drift or two to fill the pot-holes. As you drive towards Rattray Head Beach on the left you can see a row of derelict houses these were once occupied by employees of the coastguard, and then some ruined cottages, these are the remains of a village known as **'Botany Bay'**.

Botany Bay – Name given to the fishing village which once stood at **Rattray Head**. The village was established around 1795, and was officially known as the 'Seatown of Rattray', however it was very quickly nick-named 'Botany Bay' after the desolate penal colony in Australia, which itself was earlier established in 1788. The remoteness of the location being the similarity between the two places, even though they are on the opposite sides of the world. Today we can still sense the remoteness at Rattray Head, it's very common to visit the beach and be the only person for miles. The village developed from 1803 when locals took residence there, and fishermen from **Boatlea** arrived. The remoteness of the area took its toll on the new-comers particularly the fishermen, even though the sea was plentiful with fish they found it hard to scrape an existence due to the dangerous waters and inclement weather, and by the 1830's many had had enough and left. In 1838 the land-owners advertised for fishermen to come to the village and a bit of a resurgence occurred, however these new-comers met the same problems as the earlier inhabitants and struggled to survive, however the village did have occupants until the mid 1900's, today all that remains is ruins and rubble. Grid Ref NK100580.

Rattray Head – The lighthouse was designed by Alan Stephenson and built between 1892 and 1895, it stands 120 feet high, built in two parts, the lower part contains the foghorn and the engine room and the upper part the Keeper's accommodation and the lamp. This was the first ever lighthouse to have the foghorn installed inside the lighthouse structure. The light was a five wick paraffin lamp with 44,000 candle power, Buchanness Lighthouse a little further south at the time had only 6,500 candle power. In 1982 the lighthouse keepers were withdrawn when the light was made fully automatic. The sea at this corner of Buchan is notorious for rapid tidal currents, high and dangerous seas and prior to the lighthouse being built many a ship met its fate on this shore. Grid Ref NK111578.

Rattray Head Lighthouse.

Rattray Head Beach and Lighthouse.

44

Shipwrecks – We near the end of our journey, where many a ship has ended its journey by being smashed against the shore by a cruel sea. In the days of sailing ships many came a cropper here due to the strong winds and currents, and the remains of a few can still be seen at low tide. Four can be seen at low tide within one mile south of the lighthouse.

Ribs of a shipwreck at Rattray Head Beach.

The wreck shown is thought to be the 'Excelsior' of Laurwig, a 462 GRT Norwegian barque built in 1869. She ran aground here 22nd November 1881. Her crew of thirteen were all saved.

*And from here you can see **St Fergus Gas Terminal**, for a closer look back-track to the A90, turn left and travel 2.5 mile and you'll find it, and about 1 mile further the village of **St Fergus**.*

St Fergus Gas Terminal - One of Britain's largest gas terminals, opened in 1977 by Total to receive and process gas from the Frigg field (September 1977 to 26 October 2004). The St Fergus Gas Terminal currently provides 15% of the UK's gas needs. This site is currently part-owned by Total, ExxonMobil, Shell, and Transco. The Transco terminal receives gas and distributes it to the UK's National Grid system.

St Fergus Gas Terminal.

St Fergus – The village originally known as 'Langley' was renamed St Fergus in 1616 after the ancient patron St Fergus an Irish bishop who built a basilica (An important church that has been given special ceremonial rites by the Pope) here in the first half of the 8th century. The parish at one time was included in the county of Banffshire as an annex; this was due to a legislative change by the Cheyne family land-owners who were the heritable sheriffs of Banffshire. They built 'Inverugie Castle' in the parish of St Fergus but wanted it to be under their own jurisdiction. St Fergus' ancient cemetery lies near the beach to the south east of the village. In the cemetery there is many ancient headstones showing symbols of mortality and also a sun-dial on a brick pillar dedicated to Andrew Watt a minister of the parish and his wife who both died in the 1940's, also in memory of their daughter Beatrix who died in 1979. The bell-cote was installed in the new kirk in 1868.

Headstone of William Fraser (d.1725) and his spouse Elizabeth Fraser (d.1741) St Fergus Cemetery.

Sun-dial, St Fergus Cemetery.

46

Conclusion - The Buchan coastline between Pennan and St Fergus as we find it today is generally rugged and unspoilt; in places such as Rattray Head its remoteness is unique. The coastline has cliffs, great beaches, historic places, castles, heraldry, fishing towns, villages, and a surprising amount of wildlife. This book should help you find the interesting places, and help you to enjoy your visit, and perhaps come back again, as I have done all of my life.

A' the best,
Stanley Bruce.

For more information on this stretch of coastline, and to see some more of my photographs see also:

www.webhistorian.co.uk Follow - Sites / Regional / Scotland / Banffshire Maritime Heritage Association.	Fishing boats, harbours, castles, lighthouses, wells, and much more all around the North East.
www.world66.com	Photos of the North East from Elgin to Aberdeen.
www.bbaf-arts.org.uk	'Art In The Environment' (AITE) - a selection of photos taken around Aberdeenshire.
www.heraldry-scotland.co.uk Look in Monumental Heraldry.	Heraldic panels around the North East.

I have contributed a large amount of photographs to the heraldry-Scotland website, and as a result of this I have become familiar with various family arms. Using my newly found knowledge I have researched the three sets of arms on the Fraser Mausoleum in Broad Street, Fraserburgh. In this book I have stated what I believe the arms are, however I am no expert, and it would be good if someone with more knowledge than me could confirm my findings.

Minke whale in Fraserburgh Harbour. (3 August 2007).

Map - The red roads show the route followed in this book:

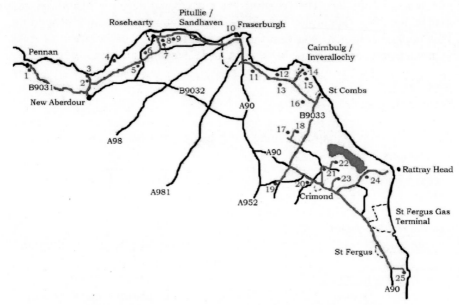

The coastline - Pennan to St Fergus. (Not to scale).

Key

1	Auchmedden Church.	14	Maggie's Hoosie.
2	St Drostan's Church.	15	Inverallochy Golf Club.
3	Aberdour Beach.	16	Inverallochy Castle.
4	Dundarg Castle.	17	Cairness House.
5	Witching Steen.	18	Lonmay Old Kirkyard.
6	Mounthooly Doo-cot.	19	Berrybrae Stone Circle.
7	Peathill Old Kirk.	20	Netherton Stone Circle.
8	Pitsligo Castle	21	Crimond Old Parish Church.
9	Pitullie Castle.	22	Loch of Strathbeg.
10	Broadsea.	23	Crimond Airfield.
11	Fraserburgh Golf Club.	24	St Mary's Chapel
12	Waters of Philorth.	25	St Fergus Old Kirkyard.
13	Cairnbulg Castle.		

See pages 21 to 32 for places not shown on the above map located within the town of Fraserburgh.